DEPARTMENT OF THE NAVY
HEADQUARTERS UNITED STATES MARINE CORPS
2 NAVY ANNEX
WASHINGTON, DC 20380-1775

I0409681

GOVERNMENT TRAVEL CHARGE CARD PROGRAM (GTCCP)

MCO 4600.40A
RFL-F
13 May 2002

MARINE CORPS ORDER 4600.40A

From: Commandant of the Marine Corps
To: Distribution List

Subj: GOVERNMENT TRAVEL CHARGE CARD PROGRAM (GTCCP)

Ref: (a) DOD 7000.14-R, DoD Financial Management Regulation,
            Volume 9, Chapter 3

Encl: (1) GTCCP Definitions
        (2) Delinquency Timeline
        (3) APC Instructions

1. Purpose. To publish guidance for GTCCP management and execution and for Cardholder participation and responsibilities in accordance with the reference.

2. Cancellation. MCO 4600.40.

3. Summary of Revision. This revision includes mandatory GTCC use as required by Public Law 105-264, Travel and Transportation Reform Act of 1998.

4. Scope. This Order applies to all service members (including Reservists) and Federal civilian employees (including wage grade employees and Non-Appropriated Fund Instrumentality employees) serving in, or employed by, the Marine Corps. This is a lawful general Order, the violation of which may be punishable under the Uniform Code of Military Justice for military members.

5. Definitions. GTCCP terms are defined in enclosure (1). Throughout this Order, the term "Commander" includes civilian supervisor equivalents. Additionally, the term "contractor" refers to the bank providing travel Card services to the Government.

6. Background. The GTCCP was initiated to limit the amount of public funds held outside the U.S. Treasury and reduce the amount of money the Government needs to borrow to fund travel advances. The GTCC provides a means of funding official travel

so that travelers do not have to request travel advances or use personal funds to travel.

7. <u>General</u>.

a. <u>Program Management</u>. The Under Secretary of Defense (Comptroller and Chief Financial Officer) has designated the Director, Defense Finance and Accounting Service (DFAS) as the DoD Program Manager. The Marine Corps Component Program Manager, HQMC (RFL), was designated by the Director, Fiscal Division, Programs and Resources Department, Headquarters, U.S. Marine Corps.

b. <u>Program Execution</u>. The Marine Corps Component Program Manager manages the overall GTCCP for the Marine Corps, implements DoD GTCC policy and oversees Intermediate Agency Program Coordinators (IAPCs). IAPCs are further responsible to their Commanders for their headquarters and subordinate command Agency Program Coordinators (APCs). Cardholder accounts are directly managed by their unit level APC.

c. <u>Mandatory Use</u>. The GTCC must be used by all Active Duty Regular and Reserve military members, and civilian personnel regardless of grade, to pay expenses arising from official Government travel, except as exempted in the reference. The Card will not be used for unfunded travel, such as permissive TAD where reimbursement for the travel would not be authorized. Current personnel and expense exemptions are as follows:

(1) <u>Personnel Exemptions</u>.

(a) Infrequent travelers (those expected to travel two or fewer times per year);

(b) Military personnel undergoing initial entry or initial skill training prior to reporting to their first permanent duty station (accession pipeline);

(c) Personnel denied a Card by the contractor, or whose Card has been canceled for financial irresponsibility or other specific reasons;

(d) Personnel who have applied for a Card but have not yet received it;

(e) Prisoners;

(f) Personnel traveling to or in a foreign country where the political, financial or communication infrastructure does not support the use of the Card;

(g) Personnel whose use of the Card due to operational or security requirements or the classified nature of the mission, poses a threat to national security, endangers the life or physical safety of themselves or others involved in the mission;

(h) Personnel traveling on invitational travel orders that do not otherwise have the Card or are not authorized to use the Card;

(i) Personnel performing separation travel upon retirement or discharge;

(j) Direct and indirect hire foreign nationals; and

(k) Individuals employed or appointed on a temporary or intermittent basis upon a determination by the individual's supervisor or other appropriate official that the duration of the employment or appointment does not justify issuance of a travel charge Card to such individual.

(2) Expense Exemptions. The following categories of travel expenses do not have to be charged to the Card, but may be if the Cardholder opts to use the Card for these expenses.

(a) Expenses incurred at a vendor that does not accept the Government-sponsored, contractor-issued travel charge Card;

(b) Laundry/dry cleaning;

(c) Parking;

(d) Local transportation system fares;

(e) Taxi fares;

(f) Tips;

(g) Local and long distance telephone calls; and

(h) Expenses covered by the "meals and incidental" portion of the per diem allowance as defined by the Joint Federal Travel Regulations (JFTR).

(3) <u>Requests for Additional Exemptions for Travelers or Expenses</u>. Requests for additional exemptions will be submitted in writing to HQMC (RFL). Exemption requests will be carefully considered, and cases recommending approval will be forwarded to the Assistant Secretary of the Navy (Financial Management & Comptroller) requesting approval. Additional exemptions will not be used until approval has been granted.

d. <u>Individually Billed Accounts (IBA)</u>. Cardholders are responsible for payment in full for the amount stated on the monthly billing statement within the terms stated on the monthly statement. The Cardholder receives the billing statement directly from the contractor at the address provided on the Card application. Cardholders are responsible for notifying the unit APC and the contractor of any contact information changes such as a new address. IBAs contain a unique prefix that identifies the account as an official Government travel Card. This prefix identifies the account as eligible for Government travel rates, including city pair rates (GSA contract airfares), and tax exemption when provided by state, county, or local law. The Card is imprinted with the words "U.S. Government, For Official Travel Only" unless a quasi-generic (plain) Card is requested by the APC for security reasons. As stated above, the quasi-generic Cards does contain the government prefix and still may therefore be considered a security concern for sensitive assignments. The following are the two types of IBAs that are available for issue:

(1) <u>Standard Card</u>. Standard Cards are issued with credit limits as established by the contractor and DoD. Information on current credit limits is contained in the reference. The APC may raise the overall credit limit and ATM cash limit with the approval of traveler's supervisor to meet mission requirements. Requests to increase ATM limits above $1,000 per month can only be approved by the Marine Corps Component Program Manager at HQMC (RFL).

(2) <u>Restricted Card</u>. Commanders may also direct issuance of restricted Cards when deemed appropriate. Restricted Cards may be issued to personnel considered a credit

risk, as determined by the Card issuer, based on credit check information. The restricted Card has a lower credit/ATM limit than a standard Card and is only activated for periods of official travel. The APC must activate a restricted Card prior to travel and deactivate it upon completion of travel. APCs can increase spending limits based on mission requirements and duration of travel.

  e. IBA Card Charges.

  (1) Mandatory Charges. Unless otherwise exempted, lodging and rental car expenses will be charged to the Card except where those goods/services are procured from a merchant that does not accept the GTCC.

  (2) Permanent Change of Station (PCS). It is Department of the Navy (DoN) policy that all PCS travelers will be advised not to use their Card for PCS or house hunting trips.

  (3) Training Expenses/Conference fees. Commands should use the appropriate training request and the purchase card vice the travel card to pay for training costs or conference fees when such fees must be paid in advance.

  (4) Other. Other official travel-related expenses that may be charged to the GTCC are emergency type expenses such as those incurred in the event of lost luggage. Such "retail" uses cannot exceed $250.00 per billing cycle for the standard Card or $50.00 for the restricted Card.

  (5) Commercial Air Transportation. Normally, commercial air transportation will be obtained through a Government-contracted commercial travel office (CTO) and charged to a centrally billed account (CBA) as described in paragraph 7.f. below. Commercial transportation may be charged to the individual Card when travel orders authorize individual procurement of commercial travel to and from the TDY site or when otherwise authorized by the Traffic Management Office (TMO). Use of the individual Card to procure commercial transportation is highly discouraged and reserved for unique situations where a Cardholder may not be able to receive commercial transportation from a CTO or a TMO.

  f. Centrally Billed Accounts (CBAs). The Government guarantees payment of CBA charges. Late payment on these accounts subjects the Marine Corps to Interest Penalties. All CBAs contain a unique prefix "448616" that indicates Government liability and identifies eligibility for Government travel rates, and tax exemption. CBAs are issued to Marine Corps Activities for the following uses:

(1) <u>Transportation Accounts</u>. CBAs are issued to TMOs to purchase airline, bus, and rail tickets. These purchases are made through a CTO, which acts as an agent for the TMO. The CTO receives an electronic invoice of transactions from the Card contractor while the TMO receives a hard-copy monthly invoice from the bank. The CTO reconciles their transaction data against the contractor's transaction data and forwards the reconciled transaction data to the TMO. The TMO reconciles that transaction data against the hard-copy invoice and sends the approved invoice to the designated payment office. Requests for transportation accounts will be submitted to HQMC (LPD-2).

(2) <u>Unit Travel Cards</u>. Unit travel Cards are issued to an individual, but charges are invoiced to the unit. The unit is liable for payment of the invoice. Unit Cards will only be used for travel expenses that would normally be charged to the individual Card. DoD policy is to minimize the issuance of unit Cards and maximize use of individual Cards. Unit Cards should be authorized and used with extreme caution. Commanders may assign a separate APC (also known as the Designated Billing Officer for the unit Card) to administer unit Card accounts. The unit Designated Billing Officer must reconcile the unit Card invoice and submit to DFAS for payment within contract terms. When authorized by the Commander, requests for unit Cards will be submitted in writing (with justification) to the Marine Corps Component Program Manager for consideration.

g. <u>Electronic Accounts Government Ledger System (EAGLS)</u>. EAGLS is a web-based management program provided by the contractor that gives the APC the ability to make account inquiries, produce monthly reports, perform Card maintenance functions, and activate/deactivate Cards. EAGLS provides near real-time update capability. Enclosure (3) contains information on electronic report generation from EAGLS. APCs can authorize Cardholders access to EAGLS to review their own account information.

h. <u>Travel Card Applications</u>. Applications must include the applicant's name, social security number, current address, work/home phone numbers, the applicant's authorization for a contractor-performed credit check, applicant's signature and supervisor/Commander approval. An application must be filled out completely or the contractor will not process it. The APC must complete the application with the appropriate central account number and hierarchy numbers and sign the application prior to submission to the contractor. New Card applicants will be required to read the contractor Cardholder agreement and sign a DoD Statement of Understanding (SOU) as shown in enclosure (3). APCs should emphasize to Cardholders that the terms of the application include an agreement to pay the account in full upon receipt of a statement.

    i. <u>Unit Check-In/Check-Out Procedures</u>. Unit procedures must direct individuals checking in or out of a command/unit to go through the APC. Detailed APC procedures are contained in enclosure (3).

    j. <u>Split Disbursement</u>. Per the reference, Split Disbursement is a strongly encouraged bill payment process that allows a traveler to designate a specific amount of their travel settlement to be paid directly to the contractor to pay their GTCC bill. Split Disbursement is a traveler benefit. If appropriate amounts are sent to the contractor, travelers do not have to pay the contractor themselves. Split Disbursement speeds payment to the contractor and reduces the potential for delinquency. The residual amount of the travel settlement after Split Disbursement will be paid to the traveler.

    (1) <u>Default Split Disbursement</u>. Unless otherwise indicated on block 1 of the DD Form 1351-2 (travel claim) any charges for transportation, lodging and rental car will be paid directly to the contractor. If the traveler does not complete block 1, the servicing Disbursing/Finance Office will execute default Split Disbursement for transportation, lodging, and rental car charges. Note: If a traveler elects not to use Split Disbursement they must annotate $0.00 or the word "none" in block one of the DD Form 1351-2 and the full amount of the travel settlement will be paid directly to the traveler.

    (2) <u>Overpayment to the Contractor</u>. If the amount split disbursed to contractor exceeds the balance on the account, the Cardholder can call the contractor to request a check be issued for the credit balance or allow the credit to be applied to future charges.

    k. <u>Card Misuse or Abuse</u>.

(1) <u>Misuse</u>. Misuse of the GTCC, as defined in enclosure (1), is strictly prohibited. Military members who misuse the GTCC are subject to the full range of criminal and administrative sanctions. Civilian employees who misuse the GTCC are subject to administrative or disciplinary action in accordance with the laws and regulations governing civilian employment.

(2) <u>Abuse</u>. The GTCC is a charge Card, not a credit Card. Cardholders are not authorized to carry a balance forward. Bills are due upon receipt and must be paid in full prior to the due date on the billing statement. Failure to keep a GTCC account current is Card abuse. Accounts delinquent due to a pending travel settlement on a claim which was properly submitted prior to the point of delinquency and electing split disbursement for the delinquent amount, are not considered abuse.

(a) An account is considered delinquent at 60 days past due. Delinquency is strictly prohibited. Extended TDY (periods exceeding 30 days) does not excuse delinquency. Partial TAD settlement submissions, as described in the reference, allow the traveler to keep their GTCC account current during any periods of extended TAD.

(b) Cardholder abuse may be punishable as a violation of the UCMJ and may subject the military member to judicial or administrative disciplinary action. Civilian employees who abuse the GTCC are subject to administrative or disciplinary action in accordance with the laws and regulations governing civilian employment.

(c) APCs will make delinquency notifications to Cardholders and Commanders as shown in enclosure (3). Sample delinquency letters are also contained in enclosure (3).

(d) Cardholders whose accounts reach 90 days past due will receive a due process notification letter from the contractor. If the delinquent amount is not paid, or if a payment plan is not established prior to the point an account becomes 120 days past due, the contractor will request that DFAS initiate salary-offset. In the event a Cardholder has gone 90 days past due because their travel claim has not been paid by the Finance/Disbursing Office due to discrepancies, the APC will advise the contractor to halt salary-offset proceedings pending the settlement of the travel claim.

(e) Cardholders whose accounts are delinquent due to unresolved billing disputes should provide any documentation regarding the disputed charge to the APC for review. Accounts delinquent due to legitimate disputes are not considered cases of abuse. Cardholders, with billing disputes on their accounts, must contact the contractor's Government Card Services Unit (GCSU) to begin the dispute process immediately. Cardholders will be required to provide the contractor a written affidavit to process a dispute for any transactions on their billing statement.

8. Action.

a. Marine Corps Component Program Manager will:

(1) Manage the Program in accordance with DoD and DoN regulations and policy;

(2) Respond to and perform liaison with the DoD and DoN Program Management Offices and the contractor as required;

(3) Provide oversight and guidance to IAPCs and APCs;

(4) Ensure policy and procedural changes are publicized in a timely manner;

(5) Ensure Commanders have the means to conduct comprehensive APC training and Cardholder education (i.e., training package distribution via IAPCs);

(6) Intercede with the contractor on behalf of Cardholders or unit APCs at the request of IAPCs;

(7) Assist Commanders in the implementation of this Order as requested;

(8) Evaluate recommended changes to this Order and take action as necessary;

(9) Consider Commander requests for additional exemptions from mandatory use and forward approved requests to ASN (FM&C) for consideration;

(10) Coordinate program inspection checklists with the Marine Corps Inspector General and Marine Corps Administrative Analysis Teams (MCAAT).

b. Commanders/Supervisors will:

(1) Ensure command/unit compliance with this Order, to include monitoring delinquency reports to eliminate delinquencies;

(2) Designate/appoint APCs and alternate APCs in writing, and provide appropriate guidance relative to their responsibilities. Forward copies of the designations to the applicable Intermediate Agency Program Coordinator (IAPC) (APC at the next higher command level). Designations will include APC/alternate mailing addresses, e-mail addresses, telephone numbers, central account number and hierarchy numbers;

(a) Provide copies of IAPC appointments to the Marine Corps Component Program Manager at HQMC (RFL);

(b) Publicize APC names, telephone numbers, and e-mail addresses throughout the unit;

(3) Ensure that APCs are proactive in the performance of their duties;

(4) Include the unit APC on personnel check-in/out sheets;

(5) Provide the unit APC with monthly listings of incoming and outgoing personnel (outgoing rosters should include transfer/separation dates);

(6) Ensure that unit traveler/APC training is documented and certify APC training completion in the copy of the APC designation;

(7) Exercise Cardholder exemption authority as appropriate, e.g., for infrequent travelers;

(8) Take appropriate action when notified of Card misuse or abuse;

(9) Ensure Cardholder confidentiality (Cardholder information is subject to Privacy Act and IAPCs/APCs may be

subject to disciplinary action for improperly divulging Cardholder confidential information); and

   (10) Disseminate GTCCP information as requested by the Marine Corps Component Program Manager at HQMC (RFL).

c.   Finance/Disbursing Officers will:

   (1) Settle TDY claims within DoD standards (currently five days);

   (2) Issue travel advances for personnel not authorized a GTCC, as requested by Commander;

   (3) Reimburse travelers for authorized ATM fees and surcharges;

   (4) Settle claims to the extent possible prior to attaching discrepancy notices for traveler corrective action; and

   (5) Provide APCs with travel-related information as requested, e.g., claim settlement status.

   (6) Split-disburse the portion of the settlement related to lodging, rental car, and transportation for Cardholders who elect split disbursement or fail to complete block 1 on the DD Form 1351-2.

   d.   Inspector General, Marine Corps will: Incorporate into the Automated Inspection Reporting System, a functional area checklist to evaluate compliance with this Order.

   e.   Command Inspectors will: Incorporate a functional checklist into local command inspection programs to evaluate compliance with this Order.

   f.   Marine Corps Administrative Analysis Team will: In coordination with HQMC (RFL), maintain a functional area checklist to evaluate compliance with this Order.

9.   Credit Bureau Reporting. The contractor reserves the right to report adverse credit information to national credit bureaus on accounts that exceed 126 days past due. Adverse credit reporting on severely delinquent Cardholders can have a long

lasting negative effect on the Cardholder's ability to obtain personal credit.

10. <u>Change Recommendations</u>. Forward recommendations for changes to this Order through the chain of command, along with a point of contact, to HQMC (Code RFL).

11. <u>Reserve Applicability</u>. This Order is applicable to Reserve Component Cardholders.

12. <u>Effective Date and Implementation</u>. This Order is effective immediately. Commands must fulfill any labor relation obligations under Chapter 71 of Title 5, United States Code, prior to implementation of the policy with respect to employees represented by unions.

CHARLES E. COOK
ASSISTANT DEPUTY COMMANDANT
FOR PROGRAMS & RESOURCES
(FISCAL DIRECTOR)

DISTRIBUTION: PCN 10206016900

COPY TO: 7000110 (55)
            8145005 (2)
            8145001 (1)
            7000106 (1)
            7000099 (1)

DEFINITIONS

1. <u>Abuse/Delinquency</u>. An account is delinquent if it is not paid in full prior to 60 days from the billing date. A delinquent account, as a result of the following, is not considered Card abuse: late claim settlement, which is due to no fault of the Cardholder or which is due to claim dispute or an unresolved billing dispute as provided for in paragraph 7.k.(2)(e) of this Order. Delinquency for any other reason is considered Card abuse. See paragraph 27.

2. <u>Agency Program Coordinator (APC)</u>. The individual designated by the unit Commander/supervisor to execute the Government Travel Charge Card Program (GTCCP) on behalf of the unit Commander. APCs are responsible to the Commander/supervisor for GTCCP execution and are under the oversight of the Marine Corps Program Manager. APCs include Intermediate APCs (IAPCs). See paragraph 24.

3. <u>Automated Teller Machine (ATM) Transaction Fees and Surcharges</u>. ATM transaction fees are limited to 3% of the advance amount or $2.00, whichever amount is greater. Reimbursement is authorized for the next higher amount divisible by ten or twenty for those ATMs that only allow withdrawal in ten or twenty dollar increments. In the case of blanket or repeat travel orders, reimbursement is limited to the lesser of the settlement amount or the amount actually withdrawn. ATM surcharges are reimbursable in full.

4. <u>ATM Withdrawal</u>. An ATM withdrawal is a cash advance obtained through the use of the Card. The primary purpose of the GTCC is to "charge" official travel related expenses. ATM withdrawals result in fees to the Government and should be limited to the amount necessary to cover those expenses that do not typically lend themselves to charging as a form of payment (e.g., tolls, "fast food" meals, etc.). ATM limits are established by the contractor and DoD, and are subject to change. ATM limits are published in the reference. ATM limits can be raised by the APC up to $1,000 per billing cycle, if mission requirements dictate. The Marine Corps Program Manager must approve requests for ATM limits that exceed $1,000. APCs may arrange for travelers with recurring high cash requirements to have higher withdrawal authority while in their respective assignments. Requests for higher ATM limits will not be approved for delinquent accounts.

5. <u>Billing Statements</u>. Billing statements for the USMC are normally produced on the 26th of each month and payment in full is due upon receipt of the billing statement.

6. <u>Canceled Card</u>. A Card is canceled as a result of abuse or misuse, or at the request of an APC following individual transfer, separation, or employment termination. Canceled accounts cannot be reactivated. Cardholders with canceled accounts must reapply if the need for a Card exists. See enclosure (3) for re-application procedures.

7. <u>Card</u>. The Government-sponsored, contractor-issued charge Card provided to authorized personnel to fund official Government travel. It is a charge Card, NOT a credit Card, meaning the balance must be paid in full on a monthly basis.

8. <u>Cardholder</u>. Individual who has applied for and has received a Card.

9. <u>Card Company</u>. The Card provider for DoD contracted by the General Services Administration on behalf of the DoD to provide the Card in support of the GTCCP.

10. <u>Centrally Billed Accounts (CBA)</u>. CBAs are Card accounts, which are billed to a unit/organization rather than an individual. "Cardless" CBAs (account number only, no Card) are issued to transportation offices to procure transportation (airline, bus, rail) services. A variant called a "Unit Card," can be issued to units for cases where use of the individual Card is not practical. Unit Cards are normally issued in selected individuals' names with unique account numbers to aid in reconciliation. The Government (Cardholder's command or unit) is liable for all charges on CBAs.

11. <u>Charged-Off Account</u>. GTCC accounts are charged-off when the outstanding balance exceeds 210 days past-due. Charged-off accounts must be written-off by BOA in accordance with Federal banking regulations and are referred to collection agencies for recovery.

12. <u>Commander</u>. For the purpose of this Order, Commander is defined as the individual commanding a battalion/squadron or higher, an Inspector-Instructor unit, or an independent Marine detachment, **or** the civilian/military supervising an equivalent organization.

13. <u>Component Program Manager (CPM)</u>. The Marine Corps Component Program Manager (CPM) resides at HQMC(RFL), establishes overall guidance for APCs and Cardholders within DoD/DoN guidelines, and is responsible for management of the GTCCP throughout the Marine Corps.

14. <u>Commercial Travel Office (CTO)</u>. A commercial activity providing the full range of commercial travel reservations and ticketing services under contract and/or memorandum of understanding with the Government.

15. <u>Contractor</u>. The Card provider for DoD contracted by the General Services Administration on behalf of the DoD to provide the Card in support of the GTCCP.

16. <u>Credit Checks</u>. Credit checks are accomplished for new Card applicants with the Card applicant's written consent. Credit checks are a standard industry practice used by the contractor to determine the type of Card to be issued. Applicants may decline a credit check and still be issued a travel Card; however, that Card will be a restricted Card and cannot be upgraded to a standard Card unless the Cardholder consents to a credit check.

17. <u>Delinquency</u>. An individual is considered delinquent whenever their GTCC bill is not paid in full prior to 60 days from the billing statement date. Current billing statements for the USMC are normally produced on the 26th of each month and payment in full is due upon receipt of the monthly billing statement.

18. <u>Deployment, Group, or Unit Travel</u>. Groups of people traveling on official travel orders together, including units traveling in support of exercises, peacekeeping, disaster relief, and combat missions. Also includes field duty or maneuver training, and sea duty when troops involved are not permanently assigned to a ship.

19. <u>Electronic Funds Transfer (EFT)</u>. Payment method wherein funds are electronically transferred to an individually elected financial institution account.

20. <u>Government Card Services Unit (GCSU)</u>. The current contractor's office that provides customer service support for the GTCCP. Available for Cardholders and APCs 24hrs a day at 800-472-1424 or OCONUS call collect 757-441-4124. This number is located on the reverse of the Card. For APCs **only** 800-558-

0548 or OCONUS call collect 757-441-4022 (7am-9pm EST Monday-Friday) EMAIL:gcsuac@bankofamerica.com.

21. <u>Government Card Services Unit Technical Help Desk</u>. For EAGLS assistance call 888-317-2077. EMAIL: GCSUTHD@BankofAmerica.com or access via the World Wide Web at: www.gcsuthd.bankofamerica.com.

22. <u>Hierarchy Level (HL)</u>. Each Major Command is assigned its own unique HL number and each subordinate unit will have unique subordinate HL numbers assigned to them.

23. <u>Individually Billed Account (IBA)</u>. An IBA is a GTCC that is issued to an individual traveler. The traveler is responsible for payment in full upon receipt of the monthly billing statement.

24. <u>Intermediate APC (IAPC)</u>. An APC designated in writing by the Commander/Supervisor to execute the GTCCP on behalf of Major Commands/Major Subordinate Commands. IAPCs work in conjunction with the Marine Corps CPM to achieve a well managed/executed GTCCP in their command. Key duties include serving as a conduit to pass information from higher levels to subordinate units, keeping their Commander informed on the program within their command, as well as oversight over all subordinate unit APCs.

25. <u>Merchant Category Codes (MCC)</u>. Four-digit codes used by the Card network to describe the merchant type. DoD blocks some MCCs as a means to control inappropriate expenditures. The MCCs that are blocked by DoD are merchants that would not normally be associated with official travel expenses. If a Cardholder uses the Card at a merchant with a closed MCC the transaction will be denied. When necessary the Cardholder must contact the APC for a forced authorization. If the use of a blocked MCC is necessary to accomplish a mission, the APC should contact the Marine Corps Component Program Manager.

26. <u>Mission Critical Status</u>. Mission-critical travel is defined as travel performed by DoD personnel under competent orders and performing duties that, through no fault of their own, may prohibit the prompt payment of their outstanding travel charge Card bills. The APC, with their Commander's approval, is authorized to notify the Card contractor to advise the contractor of mission-critical status. While in mission critical status, individual travel charge Cards shall not be suspended or canceled, however they will still appear as delinquent on reports and will be subject to late fees. Any

outstanding bills, must be settled within 45 days of removal from this status. APCs must closely manage mission critical accounts to minimize late fees and preclude delinquency, cancellation, and salary-offset.

27. <u>Misuse</u>. Card use (charges and ATM withdrawals) outside authorized parameters (e.g., charging a gift for one's spouse while TDY or drawing an ATM advance while not on or preparing for official travel) or using the Card for purchases of any kind while not on official travel even if the account is kept current.

28. <u>Official Government Travel</u>. Travel conducted under authorized, written travel orders for official Government business.

29. <u>Program</u>. The Government Travel Charge Card Program (GTCCP).

30. <u>Quasi-Generic Card</u>. A Travel Card without the imprint, "U.S. Government, For Official Travel Use Only". However, the Card still contains the ""448612" prefix that identifies the account as being a Government Card. Quasi-Generic Cards are provided at APC request for security reasons.

31. <u>Salary-Offset</u>. An involuntary pay checkage to collect a delinquent Card balance. The contractor is required to send due process notification letters to Cardholders prior to initiating salary-offset. Due process notifications provide the Cardholder with detailed information regarding the outstanding balance, charges on their account, demand payment, and list the Cardholder's rights under law. Due process letters will be issued when accounts reach 90 days past due. Cardholders will have 30 days to pay their debt, establish a repayment plan, or contest the debt. If the debt is not resolved by 120 days past due the contractor will request that DFAS initiate salary offset. The authority for salary-offset is Public Law 105-264. Accounts subject to salary-offset will be subject to additional fees from DFAS and BoA. These fees are not reimbursable expenses and currently total $167.00 dollars.

32. <u>Split Disbursement</u>. Per the reference, Split Disbursement is the **strongly encouraged** payment method where a traveler can elect on their travel claim to have a portion of their travel settlement sent directly to the contractor to pay their GTCC bill.

33. <u>Suspended Card</u>. A Card will be suspended when the account is 60 days past due. A suspended Card is rejected when use is attempted, but it is not considered canceled. The respective APC, IAPC, CPM, or contractor may suspend Cards at any time when an account is delinquent or abuse/misuse is present or suspected.

34. <u>Temporary Duty (TDY/TAD)</u>. Official Government-ordered travel conducted away from the permanent duty station (includes temporary additional duty and temporary duty enroute under permanent change of station orders).

35. <u>Travel Order</u>. Authorized, written orders directing the performance of funded travel. Includes verbal orders when confirmed by authorized, written orders.

36. <u>Unit</u>. Organization whose structure is prescribed by competent authority, such as a Table of Organization and Equipment.

37. <u>Unit Card</u>. See Centrally Billed Accounts.

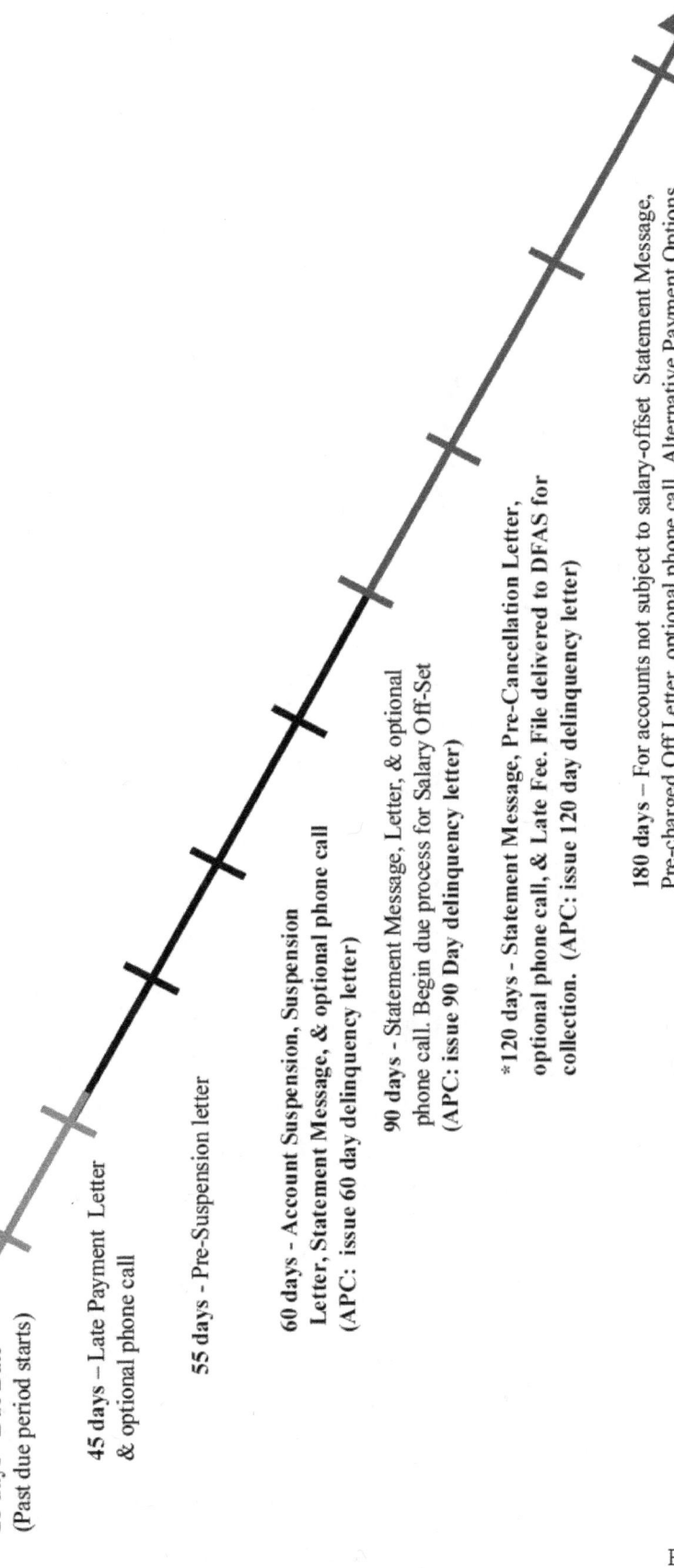

Delinquency Timeline

0 day - Account Cycles (26th of the month for USMC)

25 days - Due Date (Past due period starts)

45 days – Late Payment Letter & optional phone call

55 days - Pre-Suspension letter

60 days - Account Suspension, Suspension Letter, Statement Message, & optional phone call (APC: issue 60 day delinquency letter)

90 days - Statement Message, Letter, & optional phone call. Begin due process for Salary Off-Set (APC: issue 90 Day delinquency letter)

*** 120 days** - Statement Message, Pre-Cancellation Letter, optional phone call, & Late Fee. File delivered to DFAS for collection. (APC: issue 120 day delinquency letter)

180 days – For accounts not subject to salary-offset Statement Message, Pre-charged Off Letter, optional phone call, Alternative Payment Options Explored, Late Fees are assessed

210 days- Accounts will be written off as bad debt and reported to credit bureaus

* Accounts subject to salary-offset will be re-aged to current after 3 months of payments and will not be reported to credit bureaus

GOVERNMENT TRAVEL CHARGE CARD PROGRAM (GTCCP)
AGENCY PROGRAM COORDINATOR (APC) INSTRUCTIONS

1. <u>General</u>. These instructions must be used with the current
program material available at the Bank of America (BoA)
Technical Help Desk Web site at: www.gcsuthd.bankofamerica.com.
Training materials on compact disk (CD) can also be ordered via
the website. APCs must utilize the web site to maintain current
program information.

    a. <u>Overall Responsibilities</u>. APCs/IAPCs will operate
within the policies, procedures, and instructions established in
DoDFMR, Vol. 9 Chapter 3 (located at:
www.dtic.mil/comptroller/fmr/), this Order, and the procedures
of the contractor APC guide. Contact your IAPC or the Marine
Corps CPM for assistance if required. As an APC, you are the
principal executor of the GTCCP for your unit, the primary
liaison between the contractor bank, your Commander[1], unit
Cardholders, and your respective IAPC.

    b. <u>APC Assignment to Unit Hierarchy Account</u>. The following
12 commands are the Marine Corps HL3 IAPCs:

        COMMARFORLANT
        COMMARFORPAC
        COMMARFORRES
        COMMARFOREUR
        COMMARFORSOUTH
        COMMARCORMATCOM
        DIR AR, HQMC
        CG MCRC
        CG MCCDC
        CG MCRD Parris Island
        CG MCRD San Diego
        CG MCTFTC 29 Palms

    (1) IAPCs act as a conduit for program information flow
from the Marine Corps CPM to subordinate APCs and Cardholders.

    (2) Your Commander will designate you and your alternate
in writing. This can be done by memo. This appointment letter
must include unit hierarchy numbers and be faxed to the
contractor GCSU who will assign you in their system as an APC

---

[1]Throughout these instructions "Commander" also includes a
civilian supervisor equivalent, as applicable.

and issue you Electronic Account Government Ledger System (EAGLS) access. You cannot sign your own appointment letter (even if you have "By Direction" authority). You must also send a copy of all appointment letters to your IAPC.

(3) You must transfer every Cardholder who is a member of your unit (including civilians and members of other Services, but excluding those assigned TDY to your unit) to your account hierarchy, even if erroneously reflected elsewhere. Transfers can be effected via EAGLS, the GCSU Technical Help Desk web page, or by contacting the GCSU at 800-558-0548 or OCONUS call collect 757-441-4124. APCs must contact IAPCs for assistance in removing unidentified Cardholders from their hierarchy. IAPCs will contact the Marine Corps CPM for assistance removing Cardholders for whom a proper hierarchy cannot be identified. Unidentified Cardholders and those no longer assigned to the unit have historically represented the most serious delinquency potential. You must make resolving their status a top priority.

c. <u>Ensure Cardholder Confidentiality</u>. Cardholder information is subject to the Privacy Act and APCs/Alternate APCs may be subject to disciplinary action for improperly divulging confidential Cardholder information.

2. <u>Travel Card Applications</u>.

a. <u>Application Form</u>. Forms must be signed by the applicant, the applicant's immediate supervisor, and the APC. The applicant must also sign a Statement of Understanding (SOU) (figure 1).

b. <u>Application Processing</u>.

(1) <u>Mailing/FAX</u>. After the application is completely filled out the APC will FAX the application to the GCSU for processing. The APC will maintain a hard copy file of all applications. In cases where a FAX is not available, the original application will be mailed to the GCSU for processing. Do not sign or submit an application without an accompanying signed SOU (figure 1) and without validating the Social Security Number. After you've signed the FAX'd application, place the original SOU in your files.

(2) <u>Card Issuance</u>. Follow up with the contractor if the applicant reports the Card has not been received within two weeks. The Cardholder Personal Identification Number (PIN) is mailed separately.

ENCLOSURE (3)

2

(3) <u>Emergency Processing</u>. Expedited processing can be accomplished using FAX or overnight mail. These applications should be the exception and APCs should only mark an application "RUSH" if it is absoultely necessary. Arrangements can be made to have the Card sent to a TDY address (including to a TDY hotel, Government quarters, etc.) if requested. If faxed, do not mail the original. In these cases, maintain the original in your files. The number of emergency requests must be kept to the absolute minimum since the contractor will charge a fee (currently $20) for each expedited request. This fee is considered a reimbursable expense when the traveler submits their travel claim. The unit/command will fund the expedited request fee from their unit/command travel funds.

(4) <u>Forms</u>. Contractor forms are available at the GCSU Technical Help Desk web Page: www.gcsuthd.bankofamerica.com. Forms include: Individual Billed Account applications, account change forms, point of contact forms, etc. Blank forms may be reproduced.

3. <u>Contractor Liaison</u>.

a. <u>General</u>. As the APC, you are the liaison with the contractor for your Commander and for the Cardholders in your hierarchy. Normally, Cardholders can take care of their own matters directly with the contractor; however, they may need your help in some cases. Always intervene promptly to avoid Cardholder hardship.

b. <u>GCSU Customer Service</u>. APC liaison efforts will be conducted through the contractor GCSU currently located in Norfolk, VA at 800-558-0548, and for OCONUS call collect to 757-441-4022. The GCSU will assist in day-to-day individual account maintenance such as suspending and canceling Cards, Card replacement, account delinquency issues, etc.

c. <u>Contractor's Marine Corps Account Manager</u>. The role of the contractor's Marine Corps Account Manager is to work directly with the Marine Corps CPM and IAPCs in developing a long-term Program strategy and resolving any issues that cannot be resolved by the GCSU. APCs should always attempt to resolve issues through their IAPC and the GCSU before contacting the contractor's Marine Corps Account Manager.

4. <u>Monthly (Billing Cycle) Management Information Reports</u>.

a. <u>General</u>. **The following six reports are the minimum that unit level APCs must request and reconcile to ensure that their command's program is current.** APCs must pull these reports from EAGLS and reconcile them within 5 working days of the close of the USMC billing cycle (26th of the month). APCs must maintain copies of reports for 2 years. Copies can be maintained in hardcopy format or in electronic files. Command management control programs should incorporate reviews of reports to ensure they are maintained on file and are being worked by the APC as required by this Order. The Marine Corps Inspector General (IG) and the Marine Corps Administrative Analysis Teams (MCAAT) will also review this performance.

(1) <u>Cardholder Account Listing</u>. Provides you with a account numbers, addresses, telephone numbers, and SSNs of the Cardholders assigned to your hierarchy. The report can be pulled requesting open accounts, closed accounts, or both. **Review** the report to ensure your hierarchy is current and take appropriate action transfer accounts as necessary. If a Cardholder appears on your account who does not belong to your unit, attempt to locate the Cardholder's correct unit and have the Card moved to the appropriate hierarchy. The APC must attempt to locate the Cardholder via e-mail and notify the Cardholder that if they do not check in with their current APC within 30 days their account will be deactivated. Set up a tickler file to deactivate when 30 days have elapsed. In cases where the APC cannot locate the Cardholder's current unit, the APC will deactivate the Card to prevent any misuse/abuse and notify the CPM for assistance.

(2) <u>Account Activity Report</u>. This report reflects Cardholder activity and ATM usage during the month. **Review** the report to determine possible Card misuse and **refer** suspected misuse to your Commander in writing.

(3) <u>Pre-Suspension/Pre-Cancellation Report</u>. This report lists accounts eligible for suspension or cancellation and identifies Cardholder name, account number, status, balance past due, and number of days past due. **The key to a successful unit program is to aggressively work the pre-suspension /precancellation reports to keep accounts from being suspended or canceled.**

(4) <u>Suspension/Cancellation Report</u>. This report lists accounts that have been suspended or **canceled** and identifies account name, account number, status (suspended or canceled), date of status, balance past due, and numbers of days past due.

(5) <u>Renewal Report</u>. This report identifies Cards that are coming due for renewal since all Cards have an expiration date. APCs must review the information on this report monthly and take appropriate action. If you do nothing, Cards will be automatically renewed, so **APCs must** review this listing and take action to prevent an account from being renewed for Cardholders who have transferred, separated or terminated employment.

(6) <u>Delinquency Report</u>. This report provides a breakdown of delinquent accounts in 30 day increments, from 30 days past due through 180 days delinquent.

(7) <u>Additional Reports</u>. EAGLS has a number of other reports available that are useful Card management tools, but do not have to be worked monthly, e.g., salary-offset, ATM Cash, fixed pay, charged-off accounts). Requests for additional reports/modifications of existing reports should be submitted to the Marine Corps Component Program Manager for consideration.

5. <u>Delinquency Notifications</u>.

   a. <u>60-Day Delinquencies</u>.

   (1) **Access** EAGLS to determine if payment has been made since the report was produced. If required contact the GCSU for assistance.

   (2) **Contact** the individual. Unless the delinquency is through no fault of the Cardholder, **notify** his/her immediate supervisor in writing within five working days of report receipt. See an example notification at figure 2; E-MAIL notifications are acceptable. Cardholders are required to sign/acknowledge receipt of delinquency notifications.

   (3) Ask the Cardholder's supervisor to investigate the matter and inform you of the date the bill is paid. The contractor will normally suspend any account that is 60 days past due and then reinstate the account when the delinquent balance has been paid in full.

   (4) For Cardholders over 60 days past due because of extenuating circumstances, e.g., travel settlement problem, the APC can intercede with the GCSU and have the account annotated to that effect, especially if the Cardholder is required to travel. The GCSU can place the Card in a "Mission Critical" status and keep the Card active pending resolution of the

payment problem. **Accounts must be placed in Mission Critical status prior to reaching 60 days past due.** You must also contact the individual's personnel/administrative officer to request assistance in getting the travel claim liquidated as soon as possible.

(5) **Document** your actions and maintain file copies. The MCAAT and IG teams will review your files.

b. <u>90-Day Delinquencies</u>.

(1) If the above steps for 60-day delinquencies are followed, accounts should never reach 90 days delinquent. Contact the GCSU (or utilize EAGLS) to determine if payment has been made since the report was produced.

(2) Contact the individual. Unless the delinquency is through no fault of his/her own **notify** his/her Commander <u>in writing</u> within five working days of report receipt. See an example notification at figure 3; E-MAIL notifications are acceptable. Cardholders are required to sign/acknowledge receipt of delinquency notifications.

(3) Advise the Commander of the delinquency status. The contractor will normally suspend any account that is 60 days past due and then reinstate the account when the delinquent balance has been paid in full. Once the account reaches 75 days past due, the contractor will charge a $29 dollar late fee each month. The $29 is not reimbursable to the Cardholder.

(4) For Cardholders who are over 90 days past due on their account due to extenuating circumstances (travel settlement problem, etc.) the APC can intercede with the GCSU and have the account annotated to that effect, especially if the Cardholder is required to travel. The GCSU can place the Card in a "Mission Critical" status and keep the Card active pending resolution of the payment problem. You must also contact the individual's personnel/administrative officer to receive assistance in getting the claim liquidated as soon as possible. Impress upon the personnel officer the urgency of the situation. **Notify** the individual's immediate supervisor of any action you take, e.g., cancellation. **The Contractor will issue a due process notification letter to the Cardholder. The Cardholder will have 30 days to resolve the delinquent account, or it will be turned over to DFAS at 120 days past due for salary-offset.** If the Cardholder has not received reimbursement for properly claimed travel expenses, the APC must contact the contractor to

prevent the account from being subject to salary-offset. Salary-offset will not exceed 15% of disposable pay. Accounts referred for salary-offset will also be subject to collection fees charged by the contractor and DFAS.

(5) **Document** your actions and maintain file copies. The MCAAT and IG teams will review your files.

c. 120+ Day Delinquencies.

(1) If the above steps for 60-day and 90-day delinquencies are followed, accounts should never reach 120 days delinquent. Once accounts are over 120 days past due, a Cardholder has until the 126th day to pay the account or the account will be **canceled** by the contractor and considered "credit revoked" unless there is APC intervention and the delinquency is beyond a Cardholder's control. Cases that could be considered beyond a Cardholder's control include, but are not limited to, situations where claim settlement is delayed due to administrative error. **Accounts 120 days past due will be subject to salary-offset. Cardholders will be subject to fees as established in the reference.**

(2) If an account is **canceled** due to Cardholder negligence, the Cardholder must re-apply for a new Card. However, the contractor reserves the right to decline issuance of a new Card.

(3) If payment has not been made, unless the delinquency is through no fault of the Cardholder, **cancel** the Card. **Refer** the case in writing to the Commander for potential disciplinary/adverse personnel action. An example notification letter is provided at figure 4. Cardholders are required to sign/acknowledge receipt of delinquency notifications. **If not resolved**, continue notifications at the 150-day and 180-day marks.

(4) **Document** your actions and maintain file copies. The MCAAT and IG teams will review your files.

(5) Be aware that once an account reaches this status (126 past due), the contractor retains the right to report negative credit information to credit bureaus. Accounts on Cardholders no longer employed by the government, where salary offset cannot be applied, will be reported to credit bureaus. The contractor may also turn the account over to a collection

agency, take legal action against the Cardholder and garnish pay/salary.

(6) A Cardholder's agreement with the contractor, or the collection agency, to pay the bill in installments does not relieve him/her of potential disciplinary/adverse personnel action. As a general rule, you should not get involved in arranging for installment payments unless directed by your Commander, as this is a matter for the Cardholder to address with the contractor.

(7) **Contact** your IAPC if you need assistance.

(8) Under the contractor's current policy, accounts will not be reinstated for any Cardholder 126+ days delinquent whose account was **canceled** due to delinquency (credit revoked). Travelers whose accounts have been **canceled** due to delinquency are considered exempt from Card use per the reference and can draw a travel advance.

(9) <u>Payments</u>. Payments are applied to the most delinquent balances first. As a general rule, do not get involved in arranging partial payments unless directed by your Commander as this is a matter for the Cardholder to address with the contractor.

(10) Document your actions and maintain file copies. The MCAAT and IG teams will review your files.

6. <u>Unit Card (Centrally Billed Account) Billing Statements</u>.

a. **If** these billing statements/invoices are mailed to the command for reconciliation, **reconcile** the charges against the charge Card receipts provided by Cardholders within 5 working days of receipt of invoice.

b. **Notify** Cardholders to reimburse the command for any unauthorized expenditures or expenditures for which no receipt has been provided. A signed, written statement (with itemized expenditures) may be accepted in place of a receipt.

c. **Arrange** for Cardholder reimbursement of those items for which they received travel claim reimbursement.

d. **Sign** and **submit** the Statement of Account to the Commander for review prior to submission for payment. The

Commander will review the statement and approve for payment once charges are verified.

e. **Submit** the approved Statement of Account, claim voucher, and any monies received to the appropriate paying office for processing.

7. <u>Account Maintenance</u>.

a. <u>Cardholder Confidentiality</u>. Privacy Act restrictions apply to Cardholder account information. Cardholder files must be kept in a locked storage container/area. Documents and reports containing names and account numbers should be disposed of in accordance with local procedures for destruction of sensitive information. Cardholder delinquency information is also considered confidential, and should be treated as sensitive information

b. <u>Disputed Charges</u>. Cardholders should notify the contractor GCSU immediately in the event of any disputed charge on their billing statements. The contractor will act on behalf of the Cardholder with the vendor concerned.

c. <u>Deactivating/Suspending Cards for Other than Delinquency</u>.

(1) <u>"At Risk" Personnel</u>. Cardholders who may be under financial pressure to misuse the Card. You may deactivate standard Cards between TDY trips for those Cardholders the Commander/supervisor deems "at risk." Cards can be deactivated via EAGLS or by contacting the GCSU. Restricted Cards must be deactivated when a Cardholder is not on travel.

(2) <u>Safekeeping of Cards</u>. Since Cards are issued to individuals, it is not recommended that APCs, or any person other than the Cardholder, hold any individual's Card because of issues of availability, access, potential misuse/fraud. For Cardholders at risk of abuse/misuse, the APC should deactivate the Card. Once the Card is deactivated no charges can be made on it. For Cardholders who are separating, the APC must recover, cancel, and destroy the Card by cutting it in half and disposing of it and provide proof of cancellation to the former Cardholder.

(3) <u>Orders Issuance</u>. APCs must be included in the TDY order issuance process to ensure travelers apply for the Card

prior to travel, to activate restricted Cards when orders are issued, and to deactivate restricted Cards following completion of TDY.

    d. <u>Unit Cards (Centrally Billed Cards)</u>. You must maintain these Cards in a limited access safe as a controlled item or deactivate these Cards between TDY trips, whichever best assures the integrity of the account. Note: your unit/command is liable for all charges on these Cards.

8. <u>Merchant Category Code (MCC) Acceptance</u>.

    a. MCCs are codes used by the bank Card network to describe the merchant type. As a measure to control inappropriate Card use, DoD has directed the contractor to close a number of merchant codes that are not normally associated with official Government travel.

    b. If a Cardholder attempts to use the Card at a merchant with a closed MCC the charge will be denied. APCs can contact the GCSU for a forced authorization to allow the charges to be approved for legitimate travel charges at a closed MCC.

9. <u>ATM Withdrawal Limits</u>.

    a. <u>Limit Exceptions</u>.

        (1) <u>Decreased Limits</u>. ATM limits **may be decreased** for individuals via EAGLS or for all unit personnel by the APC making a request in writing to the contractor.

        (2) <u>Increase Limits</u>.
            (a) One-time increases up to $1,000 may be requested by APCs to support a given mission.

            (b) Requests for ATM cash limit increases in excess of $1,000 must be fowarded to the Marine Corps CPM with justification.

10. <u>Cardholder Change in Status</u>.

    a. <u>Transfer</u>. Unit personnel are required to check in and check out with the APC.

        (1) <u>Check-Out (PCS)</u>.
            (a) DoN policy is that cards will be deactivated upon PCS transfer. Instruct personnel that **they must** check-in

with their new APC at their gaining command and that if they do not do so, they will not be able to use the Card until it is moved to their new unit's hierarchy and activated. The Finance/Disbursing Office will process travel advances to fund PCS travel.

(b) Ensure you receive periodic listings of outgoing personnel and transfer dates.

(2) <u>Check-In</u>.

(a) <u>General</u>.

<u>1</u> The check-in process allows you to **transfer** the new individual's name to your hierarchy account. If you do not do so immediately, you risk the Card's cancellation by the individual's previous APC. Once canceled, the individual must go through the application process again. Make every effort to **ensure** no Cards are unnecessarily **canceled** as it creates Cardholder hardship, increased contractor costs, and additional work for you.

<u>2</u> Ensure you receive periodic new join listings.

<u>3</u> **Use** check-in as an opportunity to counsel Cardholders on authorized Card use, your role as the APC, and any Command-unique procedures. Encourage personnel to notify the contractor of their new addresses as soon as possible. This can be done through the contractor GCSU at the 1-800 number found on the back of the Card. Address changes can also be done via EAGLS by the APC or the Cardholder.

(b) <u>Statement of Understanding</u>. APCs will maintain a Statement of Understanding (SOU) (figure 1) on file for all Cardholders. Future disciplinary/or adverse personnel action is facilitated by having a signed statement on file. All newly joined personnel who already have Cards must sign new SOUs.

(c) <u>Canceled Cards</u>. New joins whose Cards were canceled at their prior command for reasons other than delinquency, must reapply unless exempted from Card use.

b. <u>Separation/Retirement/Termination of Employment</u>.

(1) **Cancel** Cards for all such individuals.

(2) **Verify** account balance via EAGLS. If the Cardholder has an outstanding balance the Commander must be informed prior to detachment.

(3) **Implement** procedures to receive periodic lists of unit personnel to keep your account current and to avoid Card misuse by former employees/Service members. The Marine Corps often has no authority over personnel who abuse the Card after separating.

(4) **Provide** the contractor with forwarding addresses if requested.

11. <u>APC Files</u>.

a. <u>Contents</u>. **Maintain** files on all Cardholder activity for which you are involved, including records of telephone calls, check-in/out, document copies, Statements of Understanding, etc. Maintain copies of Commander delegations of authority relative to this Order. **Set up and maintain** your files in accordance with SECNAVINST 5212.5D. The MCAAT and IG teams will examine/audit your files.

b. <u>Reports</u>. **Maintain** all Management Information Reports for 2 years. It is recommended that reports be maintained in electronic format to save paper and space.

12. <u>Charged-Off Accounts</u>. Accounts that reach 210 days delinquent are written off as bad debt by the contractor as required by federal banking regulations. Charged-off accounts may be reported to credit bureaus. Only accounts which the contractor is unable to initiate salary-offset will be charged-off unless paid in full prior to 210 days delinquent.

a. <u>Credit Implications</u>. If the contractor reports adverse credit information to the national credit bureaus it can have a long lasting negative effect on a Cardholders ability to obtain personal credit, e.g., car loan, home mortgage. Individuals may also be subject to higher interest rates or denied credit because they are viewed as a credit risk. Even if a Cardholder pays off the charged-off balance, the matter will still be reflected on their credit record and could impact their ability to obtain personal credit for many years.

b. APCs should ensure that all unit Cardholders are aware of the consequences of a charged-off account. Aggressively working delinquency reports, pre-suspension/pre-cancellation reports, good internal control procedures during check-in and check-out, and prompt attention in the early stages of delinquency will prevent Cardholders from reaching a charged-off status.

13. <u>Lost or Stolen Cards and Invalid Billing</u>.

    a. Cardholders must immediately contact the APC and the Government Card Services Unit (GCSU) upon discovery of a lost or stolen Card.

    b. Cardholders must immediately notify the contractor when bills include invalid charges. The contractor will intercede on their behalf and not require payment for the disputed charge during the dispute period. During this period, the amount in dispute will not be considered delinquent.

14. <u>Training</u>. The contractor's training materials for APCs are available via the technical helpdesk web site: www.gcsuthd.bankofamerica.com, and are also available upon request from the BoA GCSU. APCs must advise new Cardholders of the proper use of the Card, and ensure that current Cardholders/supervisors/Commanders are informed of policy and procedure changes to the travel Card program. It is highly encouraged that Commanders add training on the use of the GTCC to any annual training stand down programs.

Figure (1)
DEPARTMENT OF DEFENSE/USMC STATEMENT OF UNDERSTANDING
GOVERNMENT TRAVEL CARD PROGRAM

I understand that the Government Travel Card Program is designed to improve the management and control of government travel and thereby promote the efficiency of the Federal Service. I also understand that I am authorized to use the Card only for those necessary and reasonable expenses incurred by me for official travel. I will abide by these instructions issued by the Department of Defense (DoD).

The above limitation on Card usage also applies to automatic teller machine (ATM) withdrawals. The amount of cash withdrawals may not exceed $500 (standard) or $250(restricted) per billing cycle. If my account is not delinquent and my travel orders authorize a larger advance, I can request an increase in the ATM limit through the Agency Program Coordinator (APC). I will, however, charge expenses to the account wherever feasible rather than use cash withdrawals.

I understand that the issuance of this charge Card to me is an extension of the employee-employer relationship and that I am being specifically directed to:
(Card applicants must initial all the following provisions.)

- Abide by all rules and regulations with respect to the charge Card_____
- Use the charge Card only for official travel _____
- Pay all charges upon receipt of the monthly billing statement from the Charge Card Contractor _____
- Notify the APC of any problems with respect to my usage of the charge Card_____
- Notify the Card Contractor and the APC if my charge Card is lost or stolen_____
- Notify the Card Contractor if my address changes_____

I also understand that failure on my part to abide by these rules or other misuse of the Card may result in disciplinary and or administrative action being taken against me. I also acknowledge the right of the Travel Card Contractor and/or APC to revoke or suspend my travel Card privileges if I fail to abide by the terms of this agreement or the agreement I have signed with the Travel Card Contractor.

_____   _____
(Applicant's Signature)   (Supervisor's Signature)

_____   _____
(Applicant's Printed Name)   (Supervisor's Printed Name)

_____ _____
(Applicant's Series/Grade/Title) (Supervisor's Series/Grade/Title)

NOTE: The Government Travel Card application cannot be processed without this form on file.

Figure (2)
SAMPLE 60-DAY DELINQUENCY MEMORANDUM

MEMORANDUM FOR (NAME OF CARDHOLDER'S IMMEDIATE SUPERVISOR)

SUBJECT: Delinquent Government Travel Card Payment Notification - 60 Days

We have been informed by the GSA Government Travel Card Contractor that(**Cardholder's name**) is over 60 days delinquent in payment of his/her account. The total amount due is $_____.

(Provide specific information here regarding the delinquent charges, e.g., date of charge, amounts, vendor, etc.)

The Government Travel Card contract requires that all outstanding charges be paid by the date specified on the billing statement. The Travel Card Contractor has suspended Card privileges for this Cardholder. The Cardholder should be notified of this action by the command and counseled concerning the use of the Government Travel Card. Cardholders on temporary duty more than 45 days are required to submit travel vouchers for payment every 30 days if necessary to maintain their travel Card account in a current status. Split disbursement is strongly encouraged.

Non-compliance, or failure to adhere to the guidelines for the Government Travel Card, may result in disciplinary and/or administrative action in accordance with applicable statutory and regulatory provisions and, if applicable, with the Multi-Unit Master Agreement for bargaining unit employees.

The delinquent balance may be resolved by one of the following actions: (1) payment in full, (2) a reasonable explanation for the delinquency documented and submitted to the contractor through the Agency Program Coordinator, or (3) an agreed-upon repayment schedule with the Travel Card Contractor. Billing questions may be directed to the Travel Card Contractor at the number printed on the billing statement for that purpose. Additionally, at 75 days delinquent, Cardholders are subject to a $29.00 late fee per billing cycle for each and every billing cycle until the debt is resolved.

Program management questions may be directed to (**APC's name**) at extension _____.

In accordance with MCO 4600.40A, have the Cardholder sign to acknowledge receipt of this delinquent notification and return it to me with your written response, outlining the actions taken, within 5 business days.

(Signature)
Agency Program Coordinator

Cardholder acknowledgement of memorandum receipt.

_____
Name, Grade, Organization   Date

Figure (3)
SAMPLE 90-DAY DELINQUENCY MEMORANDUM

MEMORANDUM FOR SECOND-LEVEL SUPERVISOR

THROUGH: TRAVELER'S IMMEDIATE SUPERVISOR

SUBJECT: Delinquent Government Travel Card Payment Notification - 90 Days

The 90-day delinquent notification list from the Government Travel Card Contractor has been received and (**Cardholder's name**) is now 90 days delinquent in the payment of his or her account. Total amount due is $_____. The attached 60-day notification memorandum informed you that payment on the Cardholder's Government Travel Card account was delinquent.

(Provide specific information here regarding the delinquent charges, e.g., date of charge, amounts, vendor, etc.)

The Government Travel Card contract requires all outstanding charges be paid by the date specified on the billing statement. If no action is taken on this debt, the Agency Program Coordinator or the contractor may cancel the account. Meanwhile, travel Card privileges have been suspended as of (**date**). These privileges may be restored upon complete liquidation of the debt. If this debt is not resolved prior to 120 days past due, the contractor will initiate salary offset proceedings to recover the delinquent balance. The Command must notify and counsel the Cardholder concerning the delinquent account. Cardholders on temporary duty more than 45 days are required to submit travel vouchers for payment every 30 days and maintain their travel Card account in a current status. Split disbursement is highly encouraged.

Failure to adhere to the guidelines for the Government Travel Card may result in disciplinary and/or administrative action in accordance with applicable statutory and regulatory provisions and, if applicable, with the Multi-Unit Master Agreement for bargaining unit employees.

The delinquent balance may be resolved by (1) payment in full, (2) a reasonable explanation documented and submitted to the contractor through the Agency Program Coordinator, or (3) an agreed-upon repayment schedule with the Travel Card Contractor. Billing questions may be directed to the Travel Card Contractor at the number printed on the billing statement for that purpose. Program management questions may be directed to _____ (**APC's name**) at extension_____.

In accordance with MCO 4600.40A, have the Cardholder sign to acknowledge receipt of this delinquent notification and return it with your written response, outlining the actions taken, within 5 business days.

(Signature)
Agency Program Coordinator

Cardholder acknowledgement of memorandum receipt.

_____
Name, Grade, Organization   Date

Figure (4)

SAMPLE 120-DAY DELINQUENCY MEMORANDUM

MEMORANDUM FOR COMMANDER/DIRECTOR

SUBJECT: Cancellation of Government Travel Card - 120 Days Delinquent Payment
        Notification

    The 60 and 90 day delinquent notification memoranda, dated _____ and
_____respectively, notified the immediate supervisor and the Department
Director (or equivalent manager) of the past due account for Cardholder
(**name**). It has now been brought to our attention that this Cardholder has a
delinquent Government Travel Card balance of $_____ which is over 120
days past due. The Cardholder has not resolved this debt. Therefore, the
account has been canceled. The Travel Card Contractor will now refer the
account to DFAS for salary offset. Collection action may include credit
bureau notification of the employee's failure to pay.

**(Provide specific information here regarding the delinquent account and any
other information known about the individual's response to the previous
notices of delinquency.)**

    Reinstatement of the Cardholder's account requires payment of the debt
in full and approval by the Commander or Director. The Travel Card
Contractor reserves the right to deny reinstatement. Cardholders who do not
properly liquidate their Government Travel Card debts, or who use the Card
for personal purposes, also may be subject to disciplinary and/or
administrative action in accordance with applicable statutory and regulatory
provisions and, if applicable with the Multi-Unit Master Agreement for
bargaining unit employees.

Please contact (**name**) Agency Program Coordinator, on extension _____,
should further questions arise. In accordance with MCO 4600.40A, have the
Cardholder sign to acknowledge receipt of this notification and return it
with your written response, outlining the actions taken, within 5 business
days of the date of this letter.

                          (Signature)
                 Agency Program Coordinator

Cardholder acknowledgement of memorandum receipt.

_____

Name, Grade, Organization   Date